Engineering and Construction Short Contract

This contract should be used for the appointment of a contractor for engineering and construction work which does not require sophisticated management techniques, comprises straightforward work and imposes only low risks on both client and contractor

An NEC document
June 2017

The Government Construction Board, Cabinet Office UK

The Government Construction Board (formerly Construction Clients' Board) recommends that public sector organisations use the NEC contracts and in particular the NEC4 contracts where appropriate, when procuring construction. Standardising use of this comprehensive suite of contracts should help to deliver efficiencies across the public sector and promote behaviours in line with the principles of the Government Construction Strategy.

The Development Bureau, HKSAR Government

The Development Bureau recommends the progressive transition from NEC3 to NEC4 in public works projects in Hong Kong. With suitable amendments to adapt to the Hong Kong local environment, NEC4 is expected to further enhance collaborative partnering, unlock innovations and achieve better cost management and value for money in public works projects.

NEC is a division of Thomas Telford Ltd, which is a wholly owned subsidiary of the Institution of Civil Engineers (ICE), the owner and developer of the NEC.

The NEC is a suite of standard contracts, each of which has these characteristics:

* Its use stimulates good management of the relationship between the two parties to the contract and, hence, of the work included in the contract.

* It can be used in a wide variety of commercial situations, for a wide variety of types of work and in any location.

* It is a clear and simple document – using language and a structure which are straightforward and easily understood.

NEC4 Engineering and Construction Short Contract is one of the NEC suite and is consistent with all other NEC4 documents. Also available are User Guides and Flow Charts.

ISBN (complete box set) 978-0-7277-6303-7
ISBN (this document) 978-0-7277-6210-8
ISBN (Establishing a Procurement and Contract Strategy) 978-0-7277-6223-8
ISBN (Preparing an Engineering and Construction Short Contract) 978-0-7277-6225-2
ISBN (Selecting a Supplier) 978-0-7277-6234-4
ISBN (Managing an Engineering and Construction Short Contract) 978-0-7277-6236-8
ISBN (Engineering and Construction Short Contract Flow Charts) 978-0-7277-6268-9 (e-only)

First edition 1999
Second edition 2005
Third edition June 2017

British Library Cataloguing in Publication Data for this publication is available from the British Library.

Typeset by Manila Typesetting Company

Printed and bound in Great Britain by Bell & Bain Limited, Glasgow, UK

Contents

Foreword

Continuous improvement in project delivery is required to build confidence in the UK construction sector so that we can attract more investment. The Infrastructure and Projects Authority (IPA) is the government's centre of expertise for infrastructure and major projects. We sit at the heart of government, reporting to the Cabinet Office and HM Treasury.

The application of the right contract is central to the success of the overall project delivery system. The NEC suite of contracts has been in existence for over the 20 years and has linked the projects, people and processes together to create the correct environment for successful delivery.

This new and updated NEC4 contract embraces the digital changes that are happening in the construction industry, especially around BIM, which I believe will be central to creating a step change in performance. Whilst looking forward it also builds on the fundamentals required for an effective contract.

The use of NEC4 on public sector projects will help to deliver the Government Construction Strategy as we seek to improve central government's capability as a construction client to deliver further savings in the order of £1.7bn across the Government estate. The IPA looks forward to collaborating with industry to make the delivery of projects more efficient and effective.

Tony Meggs, Chief Executive, Infrastructure and Projects Authority

Infrastructure
and Projects
Authority

Reporting to Cabinet Office
and HM Treasury

Preface

NEC was first published as a new and innovative way of managing construction contracts in 1993 – some 24 years ago. It was designed to facilitate and encourage good management of risks and uncertainties, using clear and simple language.

The NEC approach to managing contracts was endorsed in "Constructing the team – The Latham Report", which was a government/industry review of procurement and contractual arrangements in the UK construction industry. This led to a second edition in 1995 incorporating the further recommendations of that review. This contract was used increasingly in the UK and overseas, and a major revision was made with the third edition in 2005.

NEC has played a part in helping the industry do things differently and better. It has done so by introducing effective project management procedures into the contract itself. These require pro-active management of risk and change, and the day-to-day use of an up-to-date programme. The range of pricing options has given Clients flexibility in the allocation of risk and the ability to share risk and manage it, collaboratively.

The NEC suite has evolved over three decades, embedding consultation responses and user feedback, and reflecting industry development, including new procurement approaches and management techniques such as alliances, management of information (BIM) and supply chain engagement. This feedback and the new procurement approaches formed the driver for the development of the next generation contracts and the launch of NEC4.

There were three key objectives in drafting NEC4:

- provide greater stimulus to good management

- support new approaches to procurement which improve contract management and

- inspire increased use of NEC in new markets and sectors.

It was to be evolution, not revolution.

Some features of NEC4 include:

- a new design build and operate contract to allow flexibility between construction and operational requirements in timing and extent

- a new multi-party alliance contract based upon an integrated risk and reward model

- new forms of subcontract to improve integration of the supply chain.

Further enhancements include:

- finalising cost elements during the contract

- incorporating a party-led dispute avoidance process into the adjudication process

- increasing standardisation between contracts and

- providing enhanced guidance to give greater practical advice to users.

NEC has always been known for its innovative approach to contract management, and this revision continues that approach. No other contract suite has had such a transformative effect on the built environment industry as NEC. It has put the collaborative sharing of risk and reward at the heart of modern procurement. It is also unique in providing a complete, back-to-back procurement solution for all works, services and supplies in any sector and any country.

NEC4 continues to set the benchmark for best practice procurement worldwide.

Peter Higgins BSc (Hons), CEng, FICE
Chair of NEC4 Contract Board

Acknowledgements

The original NEC was designed and drafted by Dr Martin Barnes then of Coopers and Lybrand with the assistance of Professor J. G. Perry then of the University of Birmingham, T. W. Weddell then of Travers Morgan Management, T. H. Nicholson, Consultant to the Institution of Civil Engineers, A. Norman then of the University of Manchester Institute of Science and Technology and P. A. Baird, then Corporate Contracts Consultant, Eskom, South Africa.

This fourth edition of the NEC suite was produced by the Institution of Civil Engineers through its NEC4 Contract Board.

The NEC4 Contract Board is:

P. Higgins, BSc (Hons), CEng, FICE (Chair)
P. T. Cousins, BEng (Tech), DipArb, CEng, MICE, FCIArb
I. Heaphy, BSc (Hons), FRICS, FCIArb, MCInstCES, MACostE
J. N. Hughes-D'Aeth, BA (Hons), MA (Cantab)
S. Rowsell, BSc, CEng, FCIHT, FICE, MCIPS

The NEC4 drafting team consisted of:

M. Garratt, BSc (Hons), MRICS, FCIArb
R. Gerrard, BSc (Hons), FRICS, FCIArb, FCInstCES
R. Hayes, BSc (Hons), MEng, CEng, MICE, MAPM
S. Kings, BSc (Hons), MRICS, MCIPS, PhD
T. Knee-Robinson, BEng (Hons), CEng, MICE, MAPM, MCIHT
J. J. Lofty, MRICS
R. Patterson, BA, MBA, CEng, MICE
B. Trebes, BSc (Hons), MSc, FRICS, FInstCES, FAPM
B. Walker, BSc (Hons), GMICE, ACIArb

Proofreading by:

P. Waterhouse, BEng (Hons), MBA, CEng, FICE, FCIArb, FCInstCES, FCMI

The Institution of Civil Engineers acknowledges the help in preparing the fourth edition given by the NEC4 Contract Board and NEC4 drafting team and the support of the following organisations in releasing their staff:

Anthony Collins Solicitors LLP
Berwin Leighton Paisner LLP
CEMAR
Costain plc
Mott MacDonald Ltd

Short Contract

A contract between

and

for

Contract Forms

Contract Data

The *Contractor's* Offer and *Client's* Acceptance

Price List

Scope

Site Information

> **Notes about the contract are printed in boxes like this one. They are not part of the contract.**

CONTRACT FORMS

CONDITIONS OF CONTRACT

1

Contract Data

The *Client's* Contract Data

The *Client* is

Name

Address for communications

Address for electronic communications

The *works* are

The *site* is

The *starting date* is

The *completion date* is

The *delay damages* are ___ per day

The *period for reply* is ___ weeks

The *defects date* is ___ weeks after Completion

The *defect correction period* is ___ weeks

The *assessment day* is the ___ of each month

The *retention* is ___ %

The United Kingdom Housing Grants, Construction and Regeneration Act (1996) **does/does** not apply?
(delete as applicable)

The *Adjudicator* is

Name

Address for communications

Address for electronic communications

Contract Data

The *Client's* Contract Data

The interest rate on late payment is ☐ % per complete week of delay.

Insert a rate only if a rate less than 0.5% per week of delay has been agreed.

For any one event, the liability of the *Contractor* to the *Client* for loss of or damage to the *Client's* property is limited to

The *Client* provides this insurance

Only enter details here if the *Client* is to provide insurance.

The minimum amount of cover for the third insurance stated in the Insurance Table is, for any one event

The minimum amount of cover for the fourth insurance stated in the Insurance Table is, for any one event

The *Adjudicator nominating body* is

The *tribunal* is

If the *tribunal* is arbitration, the arbitration procedure is

The *conditions of contract* are the NEC4 Engineering and Construction Short Contract June 2017 and the following additional conditions

Only enter details here if additional conditions are required.

Contract Data

The *Contractor's* Contract Data

The *Contractor* is

Name

Address for communications

Address for electronic communications

The *fee percentage* is   %

The *people rates* are

category of person	unit	rate

The *published list of Equipment* is

The *percentage for adjustment for Equipment* is   % (state plus or minus)

The *Contractor's* Offer and *Client's* Acceptance

The *Contractor* offers to Provide the Works in accordance with these *conditions of contract* for an amount to be determined in accordance with these *conditions of contract*.

The offered total of the Prices is

Enter the total of the Prices from the Price List.

Signed on behalf of the *Contractor*

Name

Position

Signature

Date

The *Client* accepts the *Contractor's* Offer to Provide the Works

Signed on behalf of the *Client*

Name

Position

Signature

Date

Engineering and Construction Short Contract

Price List

Entries in the first four columns in this Price List are made either by the *Client* or the tenderer.

If the *Contractor* is to be paid an amount for the item which is not adjusted if the quantity of work in the item changes, the tenderer enters the amount in the Price column only; the Unit, Quantity and Rate columns being left blank.

If the *Contractor* is to be paid an amount for the item of work which is the rate for the work multiplied by the quantity completed, the tenderer enters the rate which is then multiplied by the expected quantity to produce the Price, which is also entered.

ITEM NUMBER	DESCRIPTION	UNIT	QUANTITY	RATE	PRICE

The total of the Prices

The method and rules used to compile the Price List are

Scope

The Scope should be a complete and precise statement of the *Client's* requirements. If it is incomplete or imprecise there is a risk that the *Contractor* will interpret it differently from the *Client's* intention.

Information provided by the *Contractor* should be listed in the Scope only if the *Client* is satisfied that it is required, is part of a complete statement of the *Client's* requirements and is consistent with the other parts of the Scope.

1 Description of the *works*

Give a detailed description of what the *Contractor* is required to do and of any work the *Contractor* is to design.

2 Drawings

List the drawings that apply to the contract.

DRAWING NUMBER	REVISION	TITLE

Engineering and Construction Short Contract

Scope

3 Specifications

List the specifications which apply to the contract.

TITLE	DATE OR REVISION	TICK IF PUBLICLY AVAILABLE

4 Constraints on how the *Contractor* Provides the Works

State any constraints on the sequence and timing of work and on the methods and conduct of work including the requirements for any work by the *Client.*

Scope

5 Requirements for the programme

State whether a programme is required and, if it is, state what form it is to be in, what information is to be shown on it, when it is to be submitted and when it is to be updated.

State what the use of the *works* is intended to be at their Completion as defined in clause 11.2(1).

6 Services and other things provided by the *Client*

Describe what the *Client* will provide, such as services (including water and electricity) and ''free issue'' Plant and Materials and equipment.

ITEM	DATE BY WHICH IT WILL BE PROVIDED

Site Information

Give information about the *site* such as the ground conditions and any other information which is likely to affect the *Contractor's* work such as the position of adjacent structures.

Conditions of Contract

1. GENERAL

Actions — **10**

10.1 The Parties shall act as stated in this contract.

10.2 The Parties act in a spirit of mutual trust and co-operation.

Identified and defined terms — **11**

11.1 In these *conditions of contract*, terms identified in the Contract Data are in italics and defined terms have capital initials.

11.2 (1) Completion is when the *Contractor* has completed the *works* in accordance with the Scope except for correcting notified Defects which do not prevent the *Client* from using the *works* or others from doing their work.

(2) The Completion Date is the *completion date* unless later changed in accordance with the contract.

(3) A Corrupt Act is

- the offering, promising, giving, accepting or soliciting of an advantage as an inducement for an action which is illegal, unethical or a breach of trust or

- abusing any entrusted power for private gain

in connection with this contract or any other contract with the *Client*. This includes any commission paid as an inducement which was not declared to the *Client* before the date of the *Client's* Acceptance.

(4) A Defect is a part of the *works* which is not in accordance with the Scope.

(5) The Defects Certificate is either a list of Defects that the *Client* has notified before the *defects date* which the *Contractor* has not corrected or, if there are no such Defects, a statement that there are none.

(6) Defined Cost is the cost of the following components incurred by the *Contractor* in Providing the Works.

- People employed directly or indirectly by the *Contractor* on the *site*, calculated by multiplying each of the People Rates by the total time appropriate to that rate.

- Plant and Materials, the amount paid by the *Contractor* including, if applicable, delivery to the *site*.

- Work subcontracted by the *Contractor,* the amount paid by the *Contractor* to the subcontractor.

- Equipment on *site,* as follows.

  - For Equipment in the *published list of Equipment* calculated by applying the *percentage for adjustment for Equipment* to the rates in the *published list of Equipment* and by multiplying the resulting rate by the time for which the Equipment is required.

  - For Equipment which is not in the *published list of Equipment* calculated by multiplying open market or competitively tendered rates for that Equipment by the time for which it is required.

  - For the transport of Equipment and for Equipment which is consumed, the amount paid by the *Contractor,* to the extent that the rates do not include transport or consumables.

(7) Equipment is items provided and used by the *Contractor* to Provide the Works and which the Scope does not require the *Contractor* to include in the *works*.

(8) The Fee is the amount calculated by applying the *fee percentage* to the amount of Defined Cost.

(9) The Parties are the *Client* and the *Contractor*.

(10) The People Rates are the *people rates* unless later changed in accordance with the contract.

(11) Plant and Materials are items intended to be included in the *works*.

(12) The Price for Work Done to Date is the total of

- the Price for each lump sum item in the Price List which the *Contractor* has completed and

- where a quantity is stated for an item in the Price List, an amount calculated by multiplying the quantity which the *Contractor* has completed by the rate.

(13) The Prices are the amounts stated in the Price column of the Price List. Where a quantity is stated for an item in the Price List, the Price is calculated by multiplying the quantity by the rate.

(14) To Provide the Works means to do the work necessary to complete the *works* in accordance with the contract and all incidental work, services and actions which the contract requires.

(15) Scope is information which

- specifies and describes the *works* or

- states any constraints on how the *Contractor* Provides the Works

and is either

- in the document called Scope or

- in an instruction given in accordance with the contract.

(16) Site Information is information which describes the *site* and its surroundings and is in the document called Site Information.

Interpretation and the law	**12**	
	12.1	In the contract, except where the context shows otherwise, words in the singular also mean in the plural and the other way round.
	12.2	The contract is governed by the law of the country where the *site* is.
	12.3	No change to the contract, unless provided for by these *conditions of contract*, has effect unless it has been agreed, confirmed in writing and signed by the Parties.
	12.4	The contract is the entire agreement between the Parties.
Communications	**13**	
	13.1	Each communication which the contract requires has effect when it is received in a form that can read copied and recorded at the last address notified by the recipient for receiving communications.
	13.2	If the contract requires the *Client* or the *Contractor* to reply to a communication, unless otherwise stated in these *conditions of contract*, they reply within the *period for reply*.
The *Client's* authority and delegation	**14**	
	14.1	The *Contractor* obeys an instruction which is in accordance with the contract and is given by the *Client*.
	14.2	The *Client* may give an instruction to the *Contractor* which changes the Scope.

14.3 The *Client* gives an instruction to correct a mistake in the Price List which is

- a departure from the method and rules stated in the Price List and used to compile it or

- due to an ambiguity or inconsistency.

14.4 The *Client's* acceptance of a communication from the *Contractor* or acceptance of the work does not change the *Contractor's* responsibility to Provide the Works or liability for its design.

14.5 The *Client*, after notifying the *Contractor*, may delegate any of the *Client's* actions and may cancel any delegation. A reference to an action of the *Client* in the contract includes an action by its delegate.

Early warning   **15**

15.1 The *Contractor* and the *Client* give an early warning by notifying the other as soon as either becomes aware of any matter which could

- increase the total of the Prices,

- delay Completion or

- impair the performance of the *works* in use.

The *Client* or the *Contractor* may give an early warning by notifying the other of any other matter which could increase the *Contractor's* total cost. Early warning of a matter for which a compensation event has previously been notified is not required.

15.2 The *Contractor* and the *Client* co-operate in making and considering proposals for how the effect of each matter which has been notified as an early warning can be avoided or reduced and deciding and recording actions to be taken.

Access to the *site* and provision of services   **16**

16.1 The *Client* allows access to and use of the *site* to the *Contractor* as necessary for the work included in the contract.

16.2 The *Client* provides services and other things as stated in the Scope.

Corrupt Acts   **17**

17.1 The *Contractor* does not do a Corrupt Act.

17.2 The *Contractor* takes action to stop a Corrupt Act of a subcontractor or supplier of which it is, or should be, aware.

17.3 The *Contractor* includes equivalent provisions to these in subcontracts and contracts for the supply of Plant and Materials and Equipment.

2. THE *CONTRACTOR'S* MAIN RESPONSIBILITIES

Providing the Works   **20**

20.1   The *Contractor* Provides the Works in accordance with the Scope.

20.2   The *Contractor* does not start work which the *Contractor* has designed until the *Client* has accepted that the design complies with the Scope.

Subcontracting and people   **21**

21.1   If the *Contractor* subcontracts work, it is responsible for Providing the Works as if it had not subcontracted.

21.2   The contract applies as if a subcontractor's employees and equipment were the *Contractor's*.

21.3   The *Client* may, having stated the reasons, instruct the *Contractor* to remove a person. The *Contractor* then arranges that, after one day, the person has no further connection with the work included in the contract.

Access for the Client   **22**

22.1   The *Contractor* provides access for the *Client* and others named by the *Client* to work being done for the contract and to stored Plant and Materials.

3. TIME

Starting and Completion   30

30.1 The *Contractor* does not start work until the *starting date* and does the work so that Completion is on or before the Completion Date.

30.2 The *Contractor* submits a forecast of the date of Completion to the *Client* each week from the *starting date* until Completion.

30.3 The *Client* decides the date of Completion and certifies it to the *Contractor* within one week of the date.

30.4 The *Client* may instruct the *Contractor* to stop or not to start any work. The *Client* subsequently gives an instruction to the *Contractor to*

- re-start or start the work or

- remove the work from the Scope.

The programme   31

31.1 The *Contractor* submits programmes to the *Client* as stated in the Scope.

4. QUALITY MANAGEMENT

Tests and inspections   **40**

40.1   The *Client* and the *Contractor* carry out tests and inspections required by the Scope. If a test or inspection shows that any work has a Defect, the *Contractor* corrects the Defect, and the test or inspection is repeated.

Searching for and notifying Defects   **41**

41.1   Until the *defects date,* the *Client* may instruct the *Contractor* to search for a Defect.

41.2   The *Client* may notify a Defect to the *Contractor* at any time before the *defects date.*

Correcting Defects   **42**

42.1   The *Contractor* corrects a Defect whether or not the *Client* has notified it.

42.2   Before Completion, the *Contractor* corrects a notified Defect before it would prevent the *Client* or others from doing their work.

42.3   After Completion, the *Contractor* corrects a notified Defect before the end of the *defect correction period.* This period begins at the later of Completion and when the Defect is notified.

42.4   The *Client* issues the Defects Certificate at the *defects date* if there are no notified Defects, or otherwise at the earlier of

- the end of the last *defect correction perio*d and

- the date when all notified Defects have been corrected.

Accepting Defects   **43**

43.1   The *Contractor* and the *Client* may each propose to the other that the Scope should be changed so that a Defect does not have to be corrected. If the *Contractor* and the *Client* are prepared to consider the change, the *Contractor* submits a quotation for reduced Prices or an earlier Completion date or both to the *Client* for acceptance. If the *Client* accepts the quotation, it changes the Scope, the Prices and the Completion Date accordingly.

Uncorrected Defects   **44**

44.1   If the *Contractor* has not corrected a notified Defect within its *defect correction period*, the *Client* assesses the cost of having the Defect corrected by other people and the *Contractor* pays this amount.

5. PAYMENT

Assessing the amount due

50

50.1 The *Contractor* assesses the amount due and applies to the *Client* for payment before each *assessment day*. There is an *assessment day* in each month from the *starting date* until the earlier of

- the month after the *Client* issues the Defects Certificate and

- either Party gives notice to the other to terminate the *Contractor's* obligation to Provide the Works.

50.2 The *Contractor's* application for payment includes details of how the amount has been assessed.

50.3 If the *Contractor* submits an application for payment before the *assessment day*, the amount due at the *assessment day* is

- the Price for Work Done to Date,

- plus other amounts to be paid to the *Contractor*,

- less amounts to be paid by or retained from the *Contractor*.

50.4 If the *Contractor* does not submit an application for payment before the *assessment day*, the amount due at the *assessment day* is the lesser of

- the amount the *Client* assesses as due at the *assessment day*, assessed as though the *Contractor* had submitted an application before the *assessment day*, and

- the amount due at the previous *assessment day*.

If the *Client* assesses an amount due it gives details of the how the amount has been calculated.

50.5 If the *Contractor* has incorrectly assessed the amount due in an application made before the *assessment day*, the *Client* corrects the amount due and gives details of how the corrected amount has been calculated before payment.

50.6 The *Contractor* pays *delay damages* for each day from the Completion Date until Completion.

50.7 An amount is retained from the *Contractor* in the assessment of each amount due until Completion. This amount is the *retention* applied to the Price for Work Done to Date. The amount retained is halved in the first assessment made after Completion and remains at this amount until the *assessment day* after the Defects Certificate is issued. No amount is retained in the assessment made after the Defects Certificate has been issued.

50.8 If the *Client* requires a programme to be submitted, one quarter of the Price for Work Done to Date is retained in assessments of the amount due until the *Contractor* has submitted a first programme to the *Client* showing the information which the Scope requires.

Payment

51

51.1 A payment is made within three weeks after the *assessment day*. The first payment is the amount due. Other payments are the change in the amount due since the previous assessment. A payment is made by the *Contractor* to the *Client* if the amount due is less than the amount due in the previous assessment. Other payments are made by the *Client* to the *Contractor*.

51.2 Interest is paid if a payment is late or includes a correction of an earlier payment. Interest is assessed from the date by which the correct payment should have been made until the date when it is paid. Interest is calculated at the rate stated in the Contract Data or, if none is stated, at 0.5% of the delayed amount per complete week of delay.

51.3 Any tax which the law requires a Party to pay to the other Party is added to any payment made under the contract.

6. COMPENSATION EVENTS

Compensation   **60**
events   60.1   The following events are compensation events.

(1) The *Client* gives an instruction changing the Scope unless the change is in order to make a Defect acceptable.

(2) The *Client* does not allow access to and use of the *site* to the *Contractor* as necessary for the work included in the contract.

(3) The *Client* does not provide something which it is to provide by the date stated in the contract.

(4) The *Client* gives an instruction to stop or not to start any work.

(5) The *Client* does not work within the conditions stated in the Scope.

(6) The *Client* does not reply to a communication from the *Contractor* within the period required by the contract.

(7) The *Client* changes a decision which it has previously communicated to the *Contractor*.

(8) The *Contractor* encounters physical conditions which

- are within the *site*,

- are not weather conditions and

- an experienced contractor would have judged, at the date of the *Contractor's* Offer, to have such a small chance of occurring that it would have been unreasonable to have allowed for them.

Only the difference between the physical conditions encountered and those for which it would have been reasonable to have allowed is taken into account in assessing a compensation event.

(9) The *Contractor* is prevented by weather from carrying out all work on the *site* for periods of time, each at least one full working day, which are in total more than one seventh of the total number of days between the *starting date* and the Completion Date. In assessing this event, only the working days which exceed this limit and on which work is prevented by no other cause are taken into account.

(10) Either Party notifies the other of a correction to an assumption made for the assessment of a compensation event.

(11) An event which

- stops the *Contractor* completing the *works* or

- stops the *Contractor* completing the *works* by the Completion Date

and which

- neither Party could prevent,

- an experienced contractor would have judged, at the date of the *Contractor's* Offer, to have such a small chance of occurring that it would have been unreasonable to have allowed for it and

- is not one of the other compensation events stated in the contract.

(12) The *Client* gives an instruction to correct a mistake in the Price List.

60.2 In judging the physical conditions for the purposes of assessing any compensation event, the *Contractor* is assumed to have taken into account

- the Site Information,

- publicly available information referred to in the Site Information,

- information obtainable from a visual inspection of the *site* and

- other information which an experienced contractor could reasonably be expected to have or to obtain.

Notifying compensation events

61

61.1 The *Client* and the *Contractor* notify the other of an event which has happened or which they expect to happen as a compensation event.

61.2 If the *Client* notifies the compensation event, it also instructs the *Contractor* to submit a quotation for the compensation event. The *Contractor* submits the quotation within one week of being instructed to do so by the *Client*. If the *Contractor* notifies the compensation event, it submits a quotation with the notification.

61.3 If the *Contractor* does not notify a compensation event within four weeks of becoming aware that the event has happened, the Prices and Completion Date are not changed unless the event arises from a correction to an assumption stated by the *Client* or the *Client* giving an instruction or changing an earlier decision.

61.4 A compensation event is not notified by the *Client* or *Contractor* after the issue of the Defects Certificate.

Quotations for compensation events

62

62.1 A quotation for a compensation event comprises proposed changes to the Prices and Completion Date assessed by the *Contractor*. The *Contractor* submits details of its assessment with each quotation. If the effects of a compensation event are too uncertain to be forecast reasonably, the *Contractor* states assumptions about the compensation event in the quotation. Assessment of the compensation event is based on these assumptions. If any of them is later found to have been wrong, either Party may notify a correction to the other Party.

62.2 The *Client* replies within two weeks of the *Contractor's* submission. If the *Client* decides that an event notified by the *Contractor*

- arises from the fault of the *Contractor,*

- has not happened and is not expected to happen,

- has not been notified within the timescales set out in these *conditions of contract* or

- is not one of the compensation events stated in the contract

the *Client* notifies the *Contractor* that the Prices and Completion Date are not to be changed.

If the *Client* decides otherwise, it notifies the *Contractor* accordingly and incudes in the notice

- acceptance of the *Contractor's* quotation or

- a statement that it does not agree with the quotation and details of the *Client's* own assessment.

62.3 If the *Client* does not reply to a quotation in accordance with the contract and within the time allowed, it is treated as acceptance by the *Client* of the quotation.

62.4 If the *Contractor* does not provide a quotation which the contract requires it to submit in the time allowed, the *Client* assesses the compensation event and notifies the *Contractor* of the *Client's* assessment within one week of when it should have received the *Contractor's* quotation.

62.5   The *Client* includes details of its assessment of a compensation event when it notifies the *Contractor* of the assessment. If the effects of the compensation event are too uncertain to be forecast reasonably, the *Client* states assumptions about the compensation event in the assessment. Assessment of the compensation event is based on these assumptions. If any of them is later found to have been wrong, either Party may notify a correction to the other Party.

Assessing compensation events	**63**

63.1   For a compensation event which only affects the quantities of work shown in the Price List, the change to the Prices is assessed by multiplying the changed quantities of work by the appropriate rates in the Price List.

63.2   For other compensation events, the change to the Prices is assessed as the effect of the compensation event upon

- the actual Defined Cost of the work already done,

- the forecast Defined Cost of the work not yet done and

- the resulting Fee.

63.3   The *Client* and the *Contractor* may agree rates or lump sums to assess the change to the Prices.

63.4   The effect of a compensation event upon the Defined Cost is calculated using rates and percentages stated in the Contract Data and other amounts at open market or competitively tendered prices with deductions for all discounts, rebates and taxes which can be recovered.

63.5   If, when assessing a compensation event the People Rates do not include a rate for a category of person required, the *Client* and *Contractor* may agree a new rate. If they do not agree the *Client* assesses the rate based on the People Rates. The agreed or assessed rate becomes the People Rate for that category of person.

63.6   A delay to the Completion Date is assessed as the length of time that, due to the compensation event, Completion is forecast to be delayed.

63.7   An assessment of the effect of a compensation event made using Defined Cost

- includes risk allowances for cost and time for matters which have a significant chance of occurring and are not compensation events and

- is based upon the assumptions that

  - the *Contractor* reacts competently and promptly to the event and

  - any additional Defined Cost and time due to the event are reasonably incurred.

63.8   A compensation event which is an instruction to change the Scope in order to resolve an ambiguity or inconsistency is assessed as if the Prices and the Completion Date were for the interpretation most favourable to the *Contractor*.

63.9   Assessments for changed Prices for compensation events are in the form of changes to the Price List.

63.10   If

- the *Client* has accepted a *Contractor's* quotation,

- a *Contractor's* quotation is treated as accepted or

- the *Client* has notified the *Contractor* of a *Client's* own assessment

for a compensation event, the assessment of that compensation event is not revised except as stated in these *conditions of contract*.

7. TITLE

Objects and materials within the *site*

70

70.1 The *Contractor* has no title to an object of value or of historical or other interest within the *site*. The *Contractor* does not move such an object unless instructed to do so by the *Client*.

70.2 The *Contractor* has title to materials from excavation and demolition unless the Scope states otherwise.

8. LIABILITIES AND INSURANCE

Client's liabilities	80	
	80.1	The following are *Client's* liabilities.

- Claims and proceedings from others and compensation and costs payable to others which are due to

  - use or occupation of the *site* by the *works* or for the purpose of the *works* which is the unavoidable result of the *works*, or

  - negligence, breach of statutory duty or interference with any legal right by the *Client* or by any person employed by or contracted to it except the *Contractor*.

- A fault of the *Client* or any person employed by or contracted to it, except the *Contractor*.

- A fault in the design contained in

  - the Scope or

  - an instruction from the *Client* changing the Scope.

- Loss of or damage to Plant and Materials supplied to the *Contractor* by the *Client*, or by others on the *Client's* behalf, until the *Contractor* has received and accepted them.

- Loss of or damage to the *works*, Plant and Materials due to

  - war, civil war, rebellion, revolution, insurrection, military or usurped power,

  - strikes, riots and civil commotion not confined to the *Contractor's* employees or

  - radioactive contamination.

- Loss of or damage to the *works* after Completion except loss or damage occurring before the issue of the Defects Certificate which is due to

  - a Defect which existed at Completion,

  - an event occurring before Completion which was not itself a *Client's* liability or

  - the activities of the *Contractor* on the *site* after Completion.

- Loss of or damage to the *Client's* property, other than the *works*, unless the loss or damage arises from or in connection with the *Contractor* Providing the Works.

Contractor's liabilities	81	
	81.1	The following are *Contractor's* liabilities unless they are stated as being *Client's* liabilities.

- Claims and proceedings from others and compensation and costs payable to others which arise from or in connection with the *Contractor* Providing the Works.

- Loss of or damage to the *works*, Plant and Materials and Equipment.

- Loss of or damage to the *Client's* property, other than the *works*, which arises from or in connection with the *Contractor* Providing the Works.

- Death or bodily injury to the employees of the *Contractor*.

Recovery of costs	82	
	82.1	Any cost which the *Client* has paid or will pay as a result of an event for which the *Contractor* is liable is paid by the *Contractor*.
	82.2	Any cost which the *Contractor* has paid or will pay as a result of an event for which the *Client* is liable is paid by the *Client*.

82.3   The right of a Party to recover these costs is reduced if an event for which it was liable contributed to the costs. The reduction is in proportion to the extent that the event for which that Party is liable contributed, taking into account each Party's responsibilities under the contract.

82.4   For any one event, the liability of the *Contractor* to the *Client* for loss of or damage to the *Client's* property is limited to the amount stated in the Contract Data. The *Contractor* is not liable to the *Client* for the *Client's* indirect or consequential loss except as provided for in these *conditions of contract*. Exclusion or limitation of liability applies in contract, tort or delict and otherwise and to the maximum extent permitted in law.

Insurance cover   **83**

83.1   The *Client* provides the insurances which the *Client* is to provide as stated in the Contract Data.

83.2   The *Contractor* provides the insurances stated in the Insurance Table except any insurance which the *Client* is to provide as stated in the Contract Data.

83.3   The insurances in the Insurance Table are in the joint names of the Parties except the fourth insurance stated. The insurances provide cover for events which are the *Contractor's* liability from the *starting date* until the Defects Certificate or a termination certificate has been issued.

INSURANCE TABLE	
INSURANCE AGAINST	**MINIMUM AMOUNT OF COVER**
Loss of or damage to the *works,* Plant and Materials	The replacement cost
Loss of or damage to Equipment	The replacement cost
Loss of or damage to property (except the *works*, Plant and Materials and Equipment) and liability for bodily injury to or death of a person (not an employee of the *Contractor*) arising from or in connection with the *Contractor* Providing the Works	The amount stated in the Contract Data for any one event with cross liability so that the insurance applies to the Parties separately
Death of or bodily injury to employees of the *Contractor* arising out of and in the course of their employment in connection with the contract	The greater of the amount required by the applicable law and the amount stated in the Contract Data for any one event

9. TERMINATION AND RESOLVING DISPUTES

Termination and reasons for termination   **90**

90.1   A Party may terminate the *Contractor's* obligation to Provide the Works for a reason stated in these *conditions of contract* by notifying the other Party and giving details of the reason for terminating. After a notification to terminate has been issued, the *Contractor* does no further work necessary to Provide the Works.

90.2   Either Party may terminate if the other Party has become insolvent or its equivalent (Reason 1).

90.3   The *Client* may terminate if the *Client* has notified the *Contractor* that the *Contractor* has not stopped one of the following defaults within two weeks of the date when the *Client* notified the *Contractor* of the default.

- Substantially failed to comply with the contract (Reason 2).

- Substantially hindered the *Client* (Reason 3).

- Substantially broken a health or safety regulation (Reason 4).

90.4   The *Contractor* may terminate if

- the *Client* has not paid an amount due under the contract within thirteen weeks of the *assessment day* which followed receipt of the *Contractor's* application for it (Reason 5) or

- the *Client* has instructed the *Contractor* to stop or not to start any substantial work or all work for a reason which is not the *Contractor's* fault and an instruction allowing the work to re-start or start or removing work from the Scope has not been given within eight weeks (Reason 6).

90.5   The *Client* may terminate if an event occurs which

- stops the *Contractor* completing the *works* or

- stops the *Contractor* completing the *works* by the Completion Date and is forecast to delay Completion by more than thirteen weeks,

and which

- neither Party could prevent,

- an experienced contractor would have judged, at the date of the *Contractor's* Offer, to have such a small chance of occurring that it would have been unreasonable to have allowed for it (Reason 7).

90.6   The *Client* may terminate if the *Contractor* does a Corrupt Act, unless it was done by a subcontractor or supplier and the *Contractor*

- was not and should not have been aware of the Corrupt Act or

- informed the *Client* of the Corrupt Act and took action to stop it as soon as the *Contractor* became aware of it (Reason 8).

90.7   The *Client* may terminate for any other reason (Reason 9).

Procedures on termination   **91**

91.1   On termination, the *Client* may complete the *works*. The *Contractor* leaves the *site* and removes the Equipment.

Payment on termination   **92**

92.1   The amount due on termination includes

- an amount due assessed as for normal payments,

- the cost of Plant and Materials provided by the *Contractor* which are on the *site* or of which the *Contractor* has to accept delivery and

- any amounts retained by the *Client*.

	92.2	If the *Client* terminates for Reason 1, 2, 3, 4 or 8, the amount due on termination also includes a deduction of the forecast additional cost to the *Client* of completing the *works*.
	92.3	If the *Contractor* terminates for Reason 1, 5 or 6 or if the *Client* terminates for Reason 9, the amount due on termination also includes 5% of any excess of a forecast of the amount due at Completion had there been no termination over the amount due on termination assessed as for normal payments.
	92.4	Within thirteen weeks of termination, the *Client* assesses the final amount due. The final payment is the amount due on termination less the total of previous payments. The *Client* gives the *Contractor* details of the assessment. Payment is made within three weeks of the *Client's* assessment.

Dispute resolution	**93**	
	93.1	A dispute arising under or in connection with the contract is referred to and decided by the *Adjudicator*. A Party does not refer a dispute to the *Adjudicator* that is the same, or substantially the same, as one that has already been referred to the *Adjudicator*.

The *Adjudicator*	93.2	(1) The Parties appoint the *Adjudicator* under the NEC Dispute Resolution Service Contract current at the *starting date*. The *Adjudicator* acts impartially and decides the dispute as an independent adjudicator and not as an arbitrator.

(2) If the *Adjudicator* is not identified in the Contract Data or if the *Adjudicator* resigns or is unable to act, the Parties choose a new adjudicator jointly. If the Parties have not chosen an adjudicator, either Party may ask the *Adjudicator nominating body* to choose one. The *Adjudicator nominating body* chooses an adjudicator within four days of the request. The chosen adjudicator becomes the *Adjudicator*.

(3) The *Adjudicator* and the *Adjudicator's* employees and agents are not liable to the Parties for any action or failure to take action in an adjudication unless the action or failure to take action was in bad faith.

The adjudication	93.3	(1) A Party may refer a dispute to the *Adjudicator* if

- the Party notified the other Party of the dispute within four weeks of becoming aware of it and

- between two and four further weeks have passed since the notification.

If a disputed matter is not notified and referred within the times set out in the contract, neither Party may subsequently refer it to the *Adjudicator* or the *tribunal*.

(2) The Party referring the dispute to the *Adjudicator* includes with its referral information to be considered by the *Adjudicator*. Any more information from a Party to be considered by the *Adjudicator* is provided within two weeks of the referral. This period may be extended if the *Adjudicator* and the Parties agree.

(3) The *Adjudicator* may

- review and revise any action or inaction of the *Client* related to the dispute and alter a matter which has been treated as accepted or correct,

- take the initiative in ascertaining the facts and the law related to the dispute,

- instruct a Party to provide further information related to the dispute within a stated time and

- instruct a Party to take any other action which is considered necessary for the *Adjudicator* to reach a decision and to do so within a stated time.

(4) A communication between a Party and the *Adjudicator* is communicated to the other Party at the same time.

(5) If the *Adjudicator's* decision includes assessment of additional cost or delay caused to the *Contractor,* the assessment is made in the same way as a compensation event is assessed.

(6) The *Adjudicator* decides the dispute and informs the Parties of the decision and reasons within four weeks of the referral. This period may be extended by up to two weeks with the consent of the referring Party, or by any period agreed by the Parties.

If the *Adjudicator* does not inform the Parties of the decision within the time allowed, either Party may act as if the *Adjudicator* has resigned.

(7) Unless and until the *Adjudicator* has informed the Parties of the decision, the Parties proceed as if the matter disputed was not disputed.

(8) The *Adjudicator's* decision is binding on the Parties unless and until revised by the *tribunal* and is enforceable as a matter of contractual obligation between the Parties and not as an arbitral award. The *Adjudicator's* decision is final and binding if neither Party has notified the other within the times required by the contract that it intends to refer the matter to the *tribunal*.

The *tribunal*	93.4	A Party may refer a dispute to the *tribunal* if

- the Party is dissatisfied with the *Adjudicator's* decision or

- the *Adjudicator* did not inform the Parties of a decision within the time allowed and a new adjudicator has not been chosen,

except that neither Party may refer a dispute to the *tribunal* unless they have notified the other Party of their intention to do so not more than four weeks after

- the *Adjudicator* notifies the Parties of the decision, or, if the *Adjudicator* did not inform the Parties of the decision within the time allowed,

- the end of the time allowed for the *Adjudicator's* decision.

IF THE UNITED KINGDOM HOUSING GRANTS, CONSTRUCTION AND REGENERATION ACT 1996 AS AMENDED BY THE LOCAL DEMOCRACY, ECONOMIC DEVELOPMENT AND CONSTRUCTION ACT 2009 (THE ACT) APPLIES TO THE CONTRACT, THE FOLLOWING ADDITIONAL CONDITIONS APPLY.

Definitions

1.1 (1) In this clause, time periods stated in days exclude Christmas Day, Good Friday and bank holidays.

(2) Each *assessment day* is a payment due date. If there is a termination, the payment due date is thirteen weeks after the notice of termination.

(3) The final date for payment is three weeks after the payment due date.

Assessing the amount due

1.2 If the *Contractor* makes an application for payment before a payment due date, the application is the notice of payment specifying the sum that the *Contractor* considers to be due at the payment due date (the notified sum). The *Contractor's* application states the basis on which the amount is calculated and includes details of the calculation.

1.3 If the *Contractor* does not make an application for payment before a payment due date, the notified sum is zero or, if an amount is to be paid to the *Client*, the amount which the *Client* considers is to be paid. The *Client* notifies the *Contractor* of the notified sum.

1.4 The following replaces clause 50.5

If a Party intends to pay less than the notified sum, it notifies the other Party of its assessment of the amount due not later than seven days (the prescribed period) before the final date for payment. The notification states the basis on which the amount due is calculated and includes details of the calculation. A Party pays the notified sum unless it has notified its intention to pay less than the notified sum.

Compensation event

1.5 If the *Contractor* exercises its right under the Act to suspend performance, it is a compensation event.

The adjudication

1.6 The following replaces clause 93.3(1).

A Party may issue to the other Party a notice of its intention to refer a dispute to adjudication at any time. The Party refers the dispute to the *Adjudicator* within seven days of the notice.

1.7 The *Adjudicator* may in the decision allocate the *Adjudicator's* fees and expenses between the Parties.

1.8 The *Adjudicator* may, within five days of giving the decision to the Parties, correct the decision to remove a clerical or typographical error arising by accident or omission.

1.9 If the *Adjudicator's* decision changes an amount notified as due, payment of the sum decided by the *Adjudicator* is due not later than seven days from the date of the decision or the final date for payment of the notified amount, whichever is the later.

Index

1st Section: Index by page numbers – prefixed 'p'.

2nd Section: Index by clause numbers. (Option clauses indicated by their letters, main clause heads by bold numbers). Terms in *italics* are identified in Contract Data, and defined terms have Capital Initial Letters.